GIANTS of RAP and HIP-HOP

TRAVIS SCOTT

W.L. Kitts

ReferencePoint
Press®

San Diego, CA

About the Author

W.L. Kitts is a freelance writer and children's book author who lives in San Diego, California.

For more information, contact:
ReferencePoint Press, Inc.
PO Box 27779
San Diego, CA 92198
www.ReferencePointPress.com

LIBRARY OF CONGRESS CATALOGING-IN-PUBLICATION DATA

Name: Kitts, W. L., author.
Title: Travis Scott/by W.L. Kitts.
Description: San Diego: ReferencePoint Press, 2019. | Series: Giants of
  Rap and Hip-Hop | Includes bibliographical references and index. |
  Audience: Grades 10–12
Identifiers: LCCN 2019031452 (print) | LCCN 2019031453 (ebook) | ISBN
  9781682827734 (library binding) | ISBN 9781682827741 (ebook)
Subjects: LCSH: Scott, Travis—Juvenile literature. | Rap musicians—United
  States—Biography—Juvenile literature.
Classification: LCC ML3930.S397 K57 2019 (print) | LCC ML3930.S397
  (ebook) | DDC 782.421649092 [B]—dc23
LC record available at https://lccn.loc.gov/2019031452
LC ebook record available at https://lccn.loc.gov/2019031453

CONTENTS

THE VOICE

Travis Scott does not like to be pigeonholed. He explained to *MTV News*, "Man, I'm not hip hop. I might be an MC and a rapper, but man, I [do] this process differently," Scott said. "I don't like categories. I'm an artist. I produce. I direct, and all of that goes into the music."[1] And yet, this Texas-born rapper who *seems* to have come out of nowhere was called "the sound of hip-hop in 2019"[2] by Jeff Miers, the music critic for the *Buffalo News*. Miers is not the only one to elevate Scott in this way. Not four months earlier megastar Ellen DeGeneres introduced Scott on her talk show as "the voice of his generation."[3] The opinions of DeGeneres and Miers are based on Scott's meteoric rise to fame after his third studio album, *Astroworld*.

Out of This World

Released in 2018, *Astroworld* is Scott's most successful album to date. The album, a nod to the former Houston-area theme park that figured prominently in his childhood, achieved gold status practically upon release. It hit sales of 500,000—a sign of success in the music industry and a sales benchmark with the Recording Industry Association of America. It reached double platinum (2 million sales) six months later. *Astroworld* also earned the number two spot for highest sales during its first week. It was second only to *Scorpion*, the double album by Toronto rapper Drake. And one of *Astroworld*'s singles, "Sicko Mode,"—a collaboration with Drake—garnered Scott his first number one song on Billboard Hot 100 and went five-times platinum, selling 5 million copies. "Travis Scott has been a major name in hip-hop for a few years now," says Miers, "but for much of mainstream America, he arrived as a dynamic stranger in the middle of Maroon 5's snoozer of a Super Bowl halftime show, and then all but owned the Grammys, performance-wise, a week later. It was as if he appeared from nowhere, fully formed, Kardashian girlfriend and all."[4]

Miers is referring to Scott's televised appearances at the 2019 Super Bowl and the Grammy Awards as well as his connection to Kylie Jenner, whom he started dating in April 2017. The billionaire businesswoman and former costar of the reality television show, *Keeping Up with the Kardashians,* is the mother of Scott's daughter, Stormi Webster. And dating one of the planet's most followed people on social media can only help the young songwriter's image—an image that has already seen both the extreme highs and extreme lows of a career in the public eye.

> "It was as if [Travis Scott] appeared from nowhere, fully formed, Kardashian girlfriend and all."[4]
>
> —Jeff Miers, the music critic for the *Buffalo News*

All About the Beat

Scott has been compared by some to the hip-hop music master Dr. Dre, whose innovative sound captured a generation of fans almost three decades ago, but Scott also has some detractors in the music world. Andy Kellman, a writer with the website *AllMusic*, is one of them. He describes Scott's production-slick, club-grinding sound interspersed with staccato phrases as a "heavily Auto-Tuned half-sung/half-rapped vocal style."[5] Auto-Tune, software that helps musicians create pitch-perfect sound in their vocals as well as their equipment, is changing the sound of rap and hip-hop. Many purists of the art form do not like the produced sound, which has been steadily taking over the genre. Others have criticized Scott for what they describe as disjointed beats and sparse, impersonal lyrics that fail to tell his story. One reviewer even described Scott's music as more like a text message than a letter.

Scott has heard the criticism but brushes it off. He feels the beat and uses that as a jumping-off point for creating music. In an interview in the pop culture magazine *Complex* he explains, "My music isn't rappity-rap-rap-rap. I base my music off of lifestyle and emotion—that's why my music has a lot of chords," says Scott. "I consider myself an artist, which is, like, the most played term, but I believe it. . . . I'm not, like, super conscious. I don't write, I just go in the [recording] booth. I'm attached to the beat. The beat speaks words. I love music."[6]

It is Scott's artistry that has turned him into a rising star and has attracted iconic musicians like Stevie Wonder to be part of his projects. Zach Quiñones, a music writer for the website *Medium* who feels Scott's unique sound is part of the evolution of the genre, explains how Scott not only tapped some of the biggest hip-hop names, including Drake and The Weeknd, to contribute to *Astroworld* but also incorporated their sound into his own: "Despite the extended list of contributors, Scott elevated himself to that of a composer leading an orchestra of talent. Travis wasn't just a guy creating beats, he was an artist with a vision."[7]

> "Travis wasn't just a guy creating beats, he was an artist with a vision."[7]
>
> —Zach Quiñones, a music writer for *Medium*

Fame and Wealth

Despite Scott's insistence that he is not hip-hop, he was listed on the 2018 Hip-Hop Cash Kings list, an annual ranking by *Forbes* of the world's highest-paid hip-hop musicians. Coming in at number fifteen, Scott was estimated to have made $21 million. The magazine also chose Scott for another 2018 *Forbes* list: "30 Under 30" musical acts who are considered to be "topping charts and shifting culture."[8]

Scott's fame and wealth at such a young age is not only due to his record sales and sellout concerts. Scott also has a knack for packaging his music with limited-time-offer add-ons. For example, he designed a collectible Travis Scott action figure to be included with his first studio album, *Rodeo*. Then there is his multimillion-dollar endorsement with Nike for his own line of footwear that he designed. Scott also produces records for other big names in the industry, such as Rihanna, Drake, Jay-Z, and Kanye West. All of these endeavors have contributed to Scott's wealth and his place in hip-hop history—which is a long way from where he started, when he was practically homeless after dropping out of college to follow his music dreams.

FINDING HIS WAY

Travis Scott was born Jacques Berman Webster II in Houston, Texas. Some sources say he was born on April 30, 1991, but others list the year as 1992. His official website does not include any biographical information about him, which is very much in keeping with Scott's desire to keep his private life private. Scott rarely speaks publicly about his family, although he has given interviews in which he has mentioned that he has an older brother who is autistic and requires a full-time caregiver. He also has a younger brother and sister who are twins.

For the first six or seven years of his life, Scott and his family lived with his grandmother in South Park, a crime-ridden neighborhood in Houston. Living in this neighborhood was an experience that left a mark on young Scott. He told an interviewer, "Growing up, my grandmother stayed in the hood so I seen random crazy [stuff]," Scott said. "[I saw] mad bums and crazy spazzed out [people], I saw people looking weird, hungry, and grimy. I was always like, 'I gotta get . . . out.' It gave me my edge—[it made me] who I am right now."[9]

Concerned about violence in their neighborhood, in the late 1990s Scott's parents, Wanda and Jacques Webster, moved their family to Missouri City, a middle-class suburb of Houston. Scott quickly adapted to the new setting, which was more diverse than his old neighborhood, both culturally and financially. He attended private schools for both his elementary and middle school years. The people he met and the friends he made there showed him a different kind of life, a life that he aspired to be part of one day. "I loved private school," Scott said. "All my homies were rich. . . . That showed me a whole other taste level of life. That's when I knew, [this] is way bigger than Houston, period. Which influenced me to just like tap into other things, stylistically."[10]

Creatively Speaking

Scott had a pretty good life once his family moved to the more affluent neighborhood. He and his friends hung out at Astro-World, Houston's Disney-like theme park. He also went to movies, something he is still very passionate about today. And later he acted and sang in musicals in high school as a member of the Thespian Society. According to Chase B, a DJ who tours with Scott and who has been friends with him since they were

As a child, Scott and his friends frequently spent time at Houston-area amusement park AstroWorld (pictured). In 2018 Scott titled his third studio album Astroworld as a nod to the park.

nine, Scott was a "super-creative kid." Chase B told *Rolling Stone* magazine, "When he acted in plays, he would always be the lead—that charisma was already showing through."[11]

Scott was also very musical growing up. His musician father gave Scott his first set of drums when he was three and taught him how to make music. Scott also learned to play piano. He credits his father and his grandfather, a jazz composer with a master's degree in music composition, for his musical background. "Since he was 13, Travis Scott has been crafting songs," Kathy Iandoli writes in an *XXL Magazine* profile of Scott. "The year he turned into a teen, his dad bought studio equipment and Travis started tinkering with it, recording his first song over a Pharrell Williams beat that now escapes him. While attending [high school], he would drag his home theater system onto the back of his friend's truck to DJ parties."[12]

In those days, Scott mostly just mimicked other musicians, copying their sound as a way to learn how to make music. As he progressed, he started to strip their stuff out and insert his own beats and other sounds.

> "When [Scott] acted in plays, he would always be the lead—that charisma was already showing through."[11]
>
> —Chase B—DJ and Scott's childhood friend

He's Got the Beat

High school marked more changes for Scott. He switched from private schools to the public school system. It was the first time he had attended a public school. The students at his new high school represented a wider cross section of the Houston population than Scott had experienced at his elementary and middle schools. He later commented that being exposed to a broader mix of people helped him develop greater creativity in his music.

Scott was never someone who got into trouble in school or at home, but his growing fixation on his music led him to lose interest in school. He was looking for a way out of Missouri City so he could follow his music dreams. Before long, he was skipping classes to see some of his music idols or to meet people like Houston-based hip-hop producer Mike Dean. Dean would later help Scott develop his music career. Sometimes Scott would cut class to make beats with his friends. He and Chris Holloway, a friend from high school, formed a duo called the Graduates. They wrote, sang, produced, and published an EP (extended play) that they put on the social media platform MySpace. Music soon became Scott's biggest focus. "I started picking up beats like at 16. I got really serious at 17. That's when I put together tight beats," he told an interviewer. "I always wanted to know how to rap. I was just trying to tell my life story, trying to explain who I am."[13]

AstroWorld

Growing up, Scott and his friends spent a lot of their time hanging out at Astro-World—a Houston-area Six Flags amusement and water park that opened in 1968. The theme park was situated across the street from the Astrodome, home to the city's baseball team, the Houston Astros. In 2005, when Scott was thirteen, AstroWorld closed its doors for good, and a bit of Scott's innocence died along with it.

All these years later, Scott still talks about the fun he and his friends had on the park's rides. Scott would later try to re-create his childhood memories of AstroWorld (which is now a parking lot) for a new generation. In 2018 he named his third solo album *Astroworld*. Later that year, Scott also created what he hoped would be an annual event—the Astroworld Festival, a one-day music festival and carnival in Houston.

Although Scott was devastated by the closure of AstroWorld, it turned out to be a good thing for the fans of his music. When asked by *XXL Magazine* what he did for fun after his beloved theme park closed, Scott said, "I started making music."

Quoted in Kathy Iandoli, "Blessed Up," *XXL Magazine*, December 2016–January 2017. www.xxlmag.com.

Scott also discovered the music of various rappers whose styles would later influence his own. One of these was Cleveland rapper Kid Cudi. Kid Cudi inspired Scott—not just musically but also personally. Many famous musicians have created public personas, but Scott saw in Cudi a real person, a vulnerable person, a person who was tuned into the disillusioned youth of Scott's generation. And even more so, Scott felt Cudi knew what it was

Record producer Mike Dean (left) and Travis Scott (right) arrive for the 56th Annual Grammy Awards ceremony at the Staples Center in Los Angeles in 2014. Dean played a role in the development of Scott's music career.

like to feel lost, to be going through things like Scott was going through. Scott felt Kid Cudi's music was a good influence on him and attributes it to saving his life even, keeping him from harming himself when times were bad. "Kid Cudi was my guy," Scott explains to Lawrence Schlossman in *Complex* magazine. "If I had no weed, he was my drug."[14]

Kid Cudi's music also opened up Scott creatively and made him realize his own passion to express himself musically. Scott knew without a doubt that music was what he wanted to do with his life. He started posting his music on music blogs and calling or e-mailing producers directly, anything to get his music known. Other early rap influences included T.I., sometimes known as TIP, and Kanye West—both of whom would eventually play a big part in guiding Scott's career.

Rough Times

Scott's growing obsession with making beats started to cause a rift at home. In interviews, he has described his teen years as filled with tension between himself and his father. His father especially did not support Scott's music dreams despite having similar aspirations. Scott shared in *Complex* that his father was always yelling at him to shut off his music in his bedroom because it was too loud and was interfering with his own recording in the den. Scott's father even shut off the power to Scott's room at times. Their relationship eventually degraded to fistfights in front of Scott's friends.

And when Scott's father quit his job to pursue music full-time, there was even more tension in the Webster household—as well as hard times. Taking care of the family financially now fell solely on his mother's shoulders. She supported the family of six with a retail sales job selling phones. Her job required her to be on her feet, despite having a physical disability from a bicycle accident when she was young. "I've never seen her bend her leg," Scott said in an interview with *Rolling Stone*. "She's been on crutches my whole life. She takes medicine that [messes] with her whole state. She's had strokes. . . . And still she looked after me, my brothers, sister, my dad, putting up with my bull."[15]

Scott's mother did not want to him to pursue music any more than his father did. Both of his grandfathers had college degrees, and despite having lost interest in high school, Scott had graduated at the age of seventeen. Scott was smart; he could go far. In his parents' view, that meant going to college and getting a degree in something that had more of a future than music.

The Websters felt music was a dead-end career and that Scott would end up broke and living on the street. And in a way, they were not wrong. Scott did struggle financially when he was first starting out. But for Scott, becoming a musician was never about fame or money. Music was his passion, and he was looking for a one-way ticket out of Missouri City to somewhere he could follow his music dreams. "Mo City is, like, well-off or whatever, you can get an education, you can grow up and have kids, but it's hard . . . to make it."[16]

Scott knew he was good at making music. He knew he was made for something bigger. And he was convinced that he could make it in the music industry, even if his parents were not.

First Recording Studio

Travis Scott sacrificed a lot, including his bed, to go after his music dreams. When Scott was in high school, he turned his bedroom into a recording studio after his mother gave him a Mac computer. Scott recounted the story in a YouTube video with Britain's DJ Semtex: "I turned my bedroom into a full-blown studio. . . . I slept in a chair. . . . And I just had to do it, man, like all my friends . . . all my homies just came through and just recorded. I was just like an engineer."

Flash forward to today, Scott has taken his early experience and used it to produce some of the biggest names in the music business. His production credits include mega hip-hop and rap artists such as Kanye West, Rihanna, Drake, and Jay-Z.

Quoted in DJ Semtex, "Travis Scott Interview with DJ Semtex [EP.1]," YouTube, February 6, 2013. www.youtube.com.

University Dropout

Giving in to pressure from his parents, Scott reluctantly enrolled at the University of Texas, first in Austin and then in San Antonio. He majored in international business, which he found interesting. But his heart was not in it. He could not let music go. "If I'm going to class, I'm going to have to sit here and look at this professor that's teaching me [things] I'm not trying to hear. I want to be a . . . rapper bro. . . . I'm trying to rock crowds and have kids spazz. That's what I wanted to do. Entertain."[17] Scott recalled in an interview.

While at university, Scott and a classmate, Jason Eric, formed a music duo. They called themselves the Classmates. The duo put out a couple of rap mixtapes on MySpace. A mixtape, which is usually free, is a collection of songs that an artist releases to create awareness and build buzz for an upcoming album. A mixtape is much rougher production-wise than an album, making it much faster to put out than an album, which can take years to create.

> "Every day in college was depressing. . . . I wanted to be on an album . . . I wanted to be on stage rapping at MTV, I wanted to have the best video of the year."[18]
>
> —Travis Scott

The tapes got some attention in Scott's home state of Texas. Then, with dreams of winning Grammys and filling stadiums, Scott dropped out of college after two years. "Every day in college was depressing," he says.

I wanted to be an artist. I wanted to do this. . . . I wanted to be on an album. I wanted to put out my own [stuff]. I wanted to be on stage rapping at MTV, I wanted to have the best video of the year. I'm looking at other artists . . . and like everyone's all hyped about it. It frustrated me man, just seeing the Grammys, seeing the VMAs [Video Music Awards], and I'm in college. . . . I just had to get . . . out. It was driving me nuts.[18]

A Secret Life

Scott did not tell his parents that he had dropped out of school. In fact, he let them think he was still there while he continued to ask them for money for things like books or a new computer. Instead, he used the money they gave him to pay for things like music equipment, studio time, or to cover expenses like airline flights when he decided to move to New York City in 2011 and try to make a go of a music career.

Once he arrived in the Big Apple, Scott hooked up with his friend Mike Watts, who is now the cocreator of an influential industry blog called *IllRoots*. Scott slept on Watts's floor, and he couch surfed at other friends' places. He worked day and night recording at Stadium Red, the New York City recording studio known for producing rap stars like Eminem, West, and Jay-Z. He eventually published a song online called "Lights (Love Sick)."

Scott continued to make music and tried to get something going, but New York did not feel like a fit for him. He was running out of people to stay with and did not feel like he was making any progress. He felt Los Angeles was where he needed to be instead because he had a few industry connections there. One of those connections was Anthony Kilhoffer. Kilhoffer was a freelance sound engineer and producer. Scott had discovered his name in the credits on albums for Scott's idols Kid Cudi and West. Scott found Kilhoffer's e-mail address online and sent him some samples of his music. Kilhoffer saw something in the rapper's early music and looked at everything he sent. He was particularly impressed with his video. "He continually kept making . . . better music . . . and better video," said Kilhoffer in a 2019 interview. "Finally when I saw [the] 'Lovesick' video, I was like, 'If you're in L.A. let's sit down.'"[19] So, after only a few months in New York, Scott and a friend headed to the West Coast—courtesy of his parents, who still had no idea their money was no longer supporting their son's education.

Scott moved to Los Angeles (pictured) to try to jump-start his music career but was soon penniless and virtually homeless. He wound up sleeping on a friend's couch while waiting for his big break.

Busted

Once in Los Angeles, Scott continued his efforts to break into the music business by sharing his music on music blogs and following up with his connections. Around the same time, his parents made a surprise visit to San Antonio only to discover that Scott was no longer living there—or even in Texas.

During a phone call, Scott confessed to his parents what he had been doing, how he had been spending the money they sent him, and where he was now living. His parents reacted by first cutting off his phone and then cutting him off financially. Shortly after that, the friend Scott had gone with to Los Angeles left. "I was by myself. I had nobody and no money,"[20] he recalled.

17

With nowhere to stay in Los Angeles, Scott decided to move back home to Houston. But he was not prepared for what happened next. Upset by his career choice, convinced he was going to end up homeless, and furious about his lies, his parents kicked him out of their house. Now Scott was truly alone. He did not know where he was going to go or what he was going to do.

Friends Help Out

And once again, his friends stepped in. One friend bought Scott a plane ticket back to Los Angeles, and another offered him his couch. So, he headed back to California with renewed effort, and more than a bit of desperation, to make something happen with his music. "I couldn't be here without my friends," he told an interviewer. "I wouldn't like have a place to lay my head some nights but my friends held me down[;] that's how much they believed in me."[21] Scott's friends, and even Scott himself, had no idea what was coming. They had no idea that Scott's music career was about to bust wide open.

THE GRAND HUSTLE

Scott's hard work and hustling were starting to pay off. His music was finally starting to get noticed. When Scott arrived back at the Los Angeles airport this time, his phone exploded with texts and missed calls from one of his idols, T.I. The Atlanta-born rapper and actor had also seen Scott's video for "Lights (Love Sick)." T.I. liked what he saw and invited Scott to come by Conway Recording Studios in Los Angeles to talk. Scott was thrilled to meet T.I., who told him that he loved what Scott was doing musically and to keep it up, that he would be keeping his eye on him.

Anthony Kilhoffer, who still was not entirely sure about Scott as an artist, was captivated by Scott himself. He was especially impressed that Scott had made the "Lights (Love Sick)" video by himself. He signed on as Scott's manager. In an online interview with the website *Hypebeast*, Kilhoffer explained that Scott "looked like a star and he was acting like a star, his music wasn't that good, it was okay. It was a blatant rip off of Kanye honestly, but I showed it to some executives and they were like, 'man, this is pretty hot'. . . so I signed Travis."[22]

Scott was only nineteen when he and Kilhoffer first met. So Kilhoffer decided to take Scott under his wing. He took him around town and introduced him to people in the music industry. He even invited Scott to spend time with his family during holidays. It was also around this same time that Scott met L.A. Reid, who was the chief executive officer (CEO) of Epic Records, a prestigious music label of Sony Music Entertainment. Eventually, Scott would sign a music contract with Epic—his first of three.

CHAPTER TWO

Traveling in the inner circles of the music industry, it was not long before publishers started to contact Scott about purchasing his beats. Scott was finally making enough money to rent his own room and give up couch surfing. However, that did not last long. The guy he was renting a room from accused Scott of sleeping with his girlfriend and kicked him out. Homeless once again, Scott lived in a friend's car for a bit. But once again, a friend stepped in—Randall Medford, who goes by the nickname "Sickamore"—who would also eventually play a major role in Scott's career. Sickamore had been an A&R (artists and repertoire) manager for Atlantic Records. In that role, he had scouted and helped develop new talent. Sickamore put Scott up in a hotel. And it was at this hotel that Scott got the call that would change his life forever.

> "[Scott] looked like a star and he was acting like a star, his music wasn't that good . . . but I showed it to some executives and they were like, 'man, this is pretty hot.'"[22]
>
> —Anthony Kilhoffer, Scott's manager

The day before, Scott's manager, Kilhoffer, had left for New York to work on *Kanye West Presents Good Music Cruel Summer*—a debut compilation album. Before Kilhoffer left, he asked Scott to give him something he could show West. He took a beat that Scott was working on for his own upcoming album. Kilhoffer also planned to show Scott's "Lights (Love Sick)" video to West.

The next day, Kilhoffer called Scott from New York to say that West was in the middle of watching Scott's video for the second time and wanted to meet with him. To Scott, this was the realization of one of his biggest dreams. He could barely believe that West not only wanted to meet him, but that he was willing to fly him to New York for the meeting. So, Scott—once again—packed his bags, hopped on a plane, and crossed the country.

Idol Play

Scott was at West's New York studio for almost a week before meeting him. He filled his time working on his own music as well as playing around with the beats for *Cruel Summer*. At one point, he began to wonder whether he was ever going to meet the music legend. The day they finally did meet is a story that is carved into Scott's memory and one he shares often.

Rapper and actor T.I. (pictured), who was one of Scott's musical idols, played a key role in Scott's success. In 2013 Scott signed with T.I.'s record label, Grand Hustle Records.

West showed up at the studio and offered Scott a taco. It was covered in sour cream—something that Scott hates—but, of course, he ate it anyway because it came from West. As Scott recalls,

> First thing he gave me was a Doritos taco from Taco Bell. He gave it to me on this fancy . . . platter. . . . So I opened it and [it] was loaded with sour cream! He's like "Why aren't you eating it?" That taco was so . . . disgusting. But man, I wouldn't even notice it. Just playing him my music and just to see him nod his head even a little bit was just ill. After I stopped, he'll be like, "This . . . was dope," or "This [is] ill." It was fresh, other than that like sour cream in my . . . mouth.[23]

Scott and West hit it off immediately with their mutual love of music and production. Scott not only shared his own music with West (who gave him feedback), but he also helped out with some of West's songs.

West (whom Scott sometimes calls "Ye") would become Scott's most important mentor. West shared everything he knew about music and producing with Scott, helping to propel Scott's career even higher. "Kanye and I are good friends. He's like a big brother to me," Scott said in a 2013 interview. "He just wants me to be the greatest and really show the youth the value of production. He always tells me, 'You're the youth's Kanye West, but you're in your own form. You'll be where I am if you keep putting out the shit you do.'"[24]

Scott also got to briefly meet Kid Cudi that same day. At the time, Cudi was on West's music label G.O.O.D. (Getting Out Our Dreams) Music. He was also part of the *Cruel Summer* compilation. "I was sitting like, 'Man, I'm in the presence of 'Ye and Cudi. This is the art level where I want to be.'"[25]

"Kanye and I are good friends. He's like a big brother to me."[24]

—Travis Scott

Good Music

West flew Scott to Hawaii to work on *Cruel Summer* alongside some of the major names in the rap business, including Jay-Z. Scott was there for almost six months and coproduced several tracks on the album.

Afterward, Scott returned to Los Angeles and went back to work on his own album. He had left a beat with West—the one that Scott had sent with Kilhoffer. West liked it and had been playing around with it. Then, not long before *Cruel Summer* was to be released, West decided he wanted to include it on the album. He contacted Scott and a few others to see

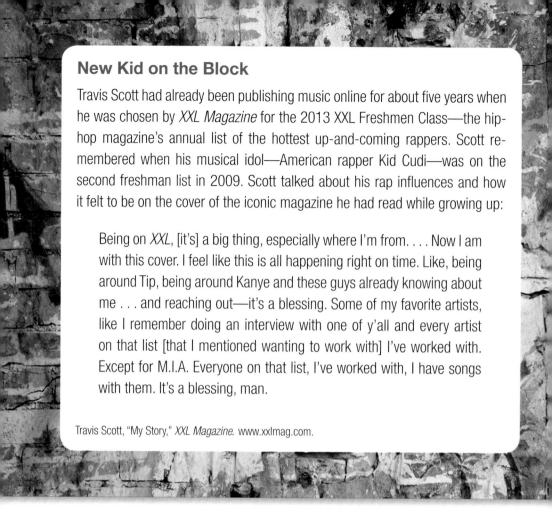

New Kid on the Block

Travis Scott had already been publishing music online for about five years when he was chosen by *XXL Magazine* for the 2013 XXL Freshmen Class—the hip-hop magazine's annual list of the hottest up-and-coming rappers. Scott remembered when his musical idol—American rapper Kid Cudi—was on the second freshman list in 2009. Scott talked about his rap influences and how it felt to be on the cover of the iconic magazine he had read while growing up:

> Being on *XXL*, [it's] a big thing, especially where I'm from. . . . Now I am with this cover. I feel like this is all happening right on time. Like, being around Tip, being around Kanye and these guys already knowing about me . . . and reaching out—it's a blessing. Some of my favorite artists, like I remember doing an interview with one of y'all and every artist on that list [that I mentioned wanting to work with] I've worked with. Except for M.I.A. Everyone on that list, I've worked with, I have songs with them. It's a blessing, man.

Travis Scott, "My Story," *XXL Magazine*. www.xxlmag.com.

whether they had any verses to go with it. Scott freestyled a verse and sent it to West. Scott's verse, along with verses from John Legend and a few others, appeared on the album as the song called "Sin City."

Cruel Summer was released in September 2012. Scott was listed as both a primary artist and a producer in the album's liner notes. It was one of the biggest albums of the year, achieving number-one status on *Billboard* magazine's charts for the top hip-hop and the top rap albums. Two months later, West offered Scott a production contract with Very Good Beats, the production side of G.O.O.D. Music.

West also flew Scott to Paris to work on West's next solo album, *Yeezus*. Scott was finally living the life that he had only dreamed of just a few years earlier in his bedroom in Missouri City. He was now working with and learning from some of the best rappers and producers in the world. With the help of West, Scott finally released two singles from *Owl Pharaoh*, a mixtape he had been working on for awhile. All Scott's hard work was beginning to pay off, and he was only twenty years old.

Two Worlds

There was yet to be another major player in Scott's career—T.I. True to his word, T.I. had been watching Scott's ascent. In April 2013, Scott signed his third music contract, this time with T.I.'s record label, Grand Hustle Records.

Scott now had access to two of the leading rappers and entertainers in the music industry. Both T.I. and West were invested in Scott—literally—and both wanted to help him go even further in his career. "They're both part of my life in this whole music [thing]," Scott told *MTV News*. "It's cool because you get the best of both worlds. You got both of these guys who are extremely super talented. I look at them as a reliable source to turn around and be like, 'Aye listen to this or aye check this out,' running it through their brains. So it's just really good having those guys around, man."[26]

Scott's star continued to rise when he was featured as an artist on the Hustle Gang's compilation mixtape, *G.D.O.D.*, which stands for *Get Dough or Die*. Shortly after, Scott released his third single from *Owl Pharaoh*, this time on the Grand Hustle label. "Upper Echelon," his debut single with his new label, featured T.I. and Tauheed Epps, the Georgia-born rapper known as 2 Chainz.

Through these compilations, including a 2014 follow-up to *G.D.O.D.*, and working on solo projects with both West and T.I.'s labels, Scott was collaborating with some of the biggest talents in rap and hip-hop. He was not only contributing as an artist and musician but also as a producer. For example, Scott has production credits on both West's *Yeezus* and Jay-Z's *Magna Carta Holy*

Grail. Both albums were released to positive reviews in mid-2013. Scott's signature sound of disjointed beats and his influence as a producer were beginning to get as much industry recognition as his own music.

Top of the Class

In May 2013, industry recognition showed up in a big way when Scott was chosen as part of *XXL Magazine*'s annual XXL Freshmen Class. Scott was featured on the cover of the hip-hop publication with the others in the 2013 "class" as one of the hottest up-and-coming rappers. Scott was making a name for himself not just within the industry but also with fans—fans who had been following Scott's music online since his early days. And this new generation of fans was looking for a change in this musical genre, along with someone to lead the evolution.

Scott's experimental music style was being compared to Dr. Dre's. Dr. Dre, a rapper and producer from Compton, California,

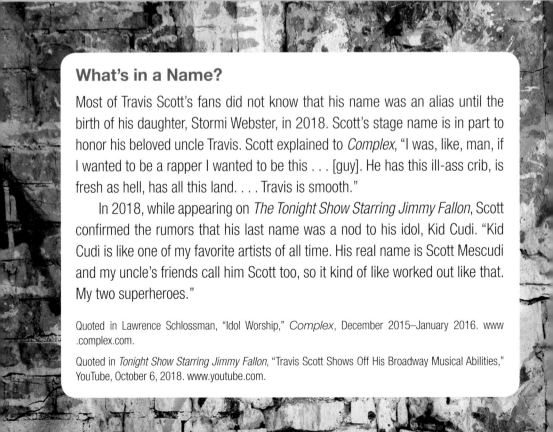

What's in a Name?

Most of Travis Scott's fans did not know that his name was an alias until the birth of his daughter, Stormi Webster, in 2018. Scott's stage name is in part to honor his beloved uncle Travis. Scott explained to *Complex*, "I was, like, man, if I wanted to be a rapper I wanted to be this . . . [guy]. He has this ill-ass crib, is fresh as hell, has all this land. . . . Travis is smooth."

In 2018, while appearing on *The Tonight Show Starring Jimmy Fallon*, Scott confirmed the rumors that his last name was a nod to his idol, Kid Cudi. "Kid Cudi is like one of my favorite artists of all time. His real name is Scott Mescudi and my uncle's friends call him Scott too, so it kind of like worked out like that. My two superheroes."

Quoted in Lawrence Schlossman, "Idol Worship," *Complex*, December 2015–January 2016. www .complex.com.

Quoted in *Tonight Show Starring Jimmy Fallon*, "Travis Scott Shows Off His Broadway Musical Abilities," YouTube, October 6, 2018. www.youtube.com.

had changed the raw sounds of rap during the 1990s, giving it a more technically produced sound. Now, almost twenty years later, millennials were looking to make changes, to claim their own sound for the musical genre—and that sound showed up with Scott's arrival on the rap scene. As music writer Zach Quiñones explains,

> "While it bared many southern rap qualities, Scott's creative direction moved into more obscure destinations that hadn't been taken advantage of in rap."[27]
>
> —Zach Quiñones, a music writer for *Medium*

> While it bared many southern rap qualities, Scott's creative direction moved into more obscure destinations that hadn't been taken advantage of in rap. His staple was combining instrumentation that wasn't considered compatible and song formats that contained sudden, unpredictable beat switches. In hindsight the parallels between Dre and Travis are more apparent, as both were conducting fearless and brash experiments with their production to lay the groundwork for the next iconic sound in Hip-Hop—restructuring the DNA.[27]

As much as Scott admired the generation of star rappers who came before him—rappers such as Jay-Z and West—he felt he had something more to offer young fans. Scott felt that being in his early twenties gave him a perspective that the older rappers lacked. Scott claimed to have his finger on the pulse of what young people wanted. And he was not afraid to make his opinions about that known. In some interviews, he commented on Jay-Z's relatively advanced age and described West as a stepfather figure to him.

Days Before Superstardom

In May 2013, after months of delays and reworking, Scott finally released his debut mixtape, *Owl Pharaoh,* as a coproduction of both Grand Hustle Records and Epic Records. In addition to

Scott, who was involved in every aspect of creating the mixtape, there were multiple producers, including West, Kilhoffer, and Scott's producer idol, Mike Dean. *Owl Pharaoh* was nominated for a 2013 Black Entertainment Television (BET) Hip Hop Award in the Best Mixtape category, and *XXL Magazine* chose it for its year-end list of the twenty-five best mixtapes.

Just over a year later, Scott followed up his success with the release of his second mixtape, *Days Before Rodeo*, a prequel to his upcoming debut album *Rodeo*. *Days Before Rodeo* was also on the Grand Hustle label and had a similar impressive list of contributors, both artists and producers. And like *Owl Pharaoh* before it, this mixtape was also released to positive reviews and was nominated for a BET award. *Days Before Rodeo* generated a 95 percent user rating on HotNewHipHop.com, a hip-hop website where artists can post their music to connect directly with fans. Scott's reputation as the voice of a new generation of hip-hop lovers was cemented.

Scott continued to build on his early success. By 2015, he was in demand as a producer working on albums for superstars such as Drake, Madonna, and Rihanna. He also cowrote the song recorded by Rihanna, "Bitch Better Have My Money." This was also the year that Scott started touring. Kilhoffer, Scott's manager, helped Scott retain a renowned hip-hop agent. The agent booked gigs for Scott at clubs and as an opening act for other, more established artists, such as The Weeknd and Rihanna. And to promote his soon-to-be-released album, Scott kicked off his month-long Rodeo Tour in March 2015 with DJ Metro Boomin and Young Thug, both of whom contributed to *Rodeo*.

Scott quickly got a reputation for putting on electric shows complete with mosh pits and whipping the crowd into a pulsing frenzy. Frazier Tharpe, a writer for *Complex*, summed up the concert's atmosphere with the title of his article: "I Tried Not to Die at Travi$ Scott and Young Thug's Show Last Night." (By

this time, some media had adopted the use of the dollar sign in Scott's first name.) Tharpe writes that the "Rodeo Tour wasn't just watching a show—it was going the distance. A turnt-up fight for survival. An environment where fans jettisoned the usual too cool for school aura that comes with rap and instead aimed to get downright rowdy on some punk."[28]

Crazed fans and sellout shows were just the tip of the proverbial iceberg for Scott. The young rapper's star was about to rise to a level only seen by a handful of entertainers in the music industry. Travis Scott had come a long way from sleeping on floors and living in a car.

ASTRONOMICAL SUCCESS

Travis Scott enjoyed increasing success throughout 2015. He was steadily gaining fans and growing his followers on social media, and he was about to release his first studio album. For that album, called *Rodeo*, Scott wanted to communicate the feeling one gets when attending a carnival or a rodeo like the ones he grew up with in Houston. Even before the album came out, it was already getting a lot of buzz. During an interview with *Billboard*, T.I. compared *Rodeo* to the albums of another young rapper—Kendrick Lamar. "It's probably going to be one of the most talked about projects and probably one of the most highly revered solo albums probably since Kendrick," T.I. asserted. "Not in the same vein as Kendrick, but just in a whole other badass, rebellious . . . way."[29]

Scott was torn, however. He had been dreaming about doing an album since his school days. And now that the moment was here, he did not want to release it without a collaboration with his childhood idol, Kid Cudi. He told *MTV News*, "I feel like he's part of my story. There would be no Travi$ Scott if it wasn't for him."[30]

While Scott was in the studio working on *Rodeo*, Cudi showed up one day. It was a complete surprise. The two hung out for the first time; they talked about all kinds of things. Scott said he cried because he was so overcome with emotion. "It was one of those moments. I felt like my life was complete."[31]

However, the musical pairing Scott had hoped for did not happen; after several delays, *Rodeo* was finally released in September 2015. It did include several other guest artists, including the Weeknd, Justin Bieber, and Kanye West. It debuted in the number-one spot for *Billboard*'s top rap albums chart and number three on the Billboard 200. The latter ranks the top two hundred albums in the United States each week by sales and livestreams across all musical genres.

Scott also put out two singles in advance of *Rodeo*'s release. One of them, "Antidote," peaked at number sixteen for the week on the Billboard Hot 100 list, which charts a single's sales, streaming, and radio play. "Antidote" eventually reached quadruple platinum status.

Same Old Story

Although *Rodeo* made several year-end best album lists, including *Complex*'s Top 25 Albums for 2015, some reviewers continued to fault both Scott's musical style and his lyrics. They criticized his rapid-fire phrases over the top of distorted instrumentation. The repetitive and disjointed phrases told fans nothing about the singer, his life, or his values. As one critic noted,

> The thought was once Travi$ Scott released his debut album, we would know more about this mysterious artist out of Mo City, one virtually unknown when he received a major co-sign from Kanye West back in 2012. That notion never comes to fruition on Rodeo, but it's not that big of a distraction. What Travi$ provides here is what he always has: a soundtrack for the restless youth who live off an emotional high. We're no more closer to the man Jacques Webster on Rodeo than we were when he set the streets ablaze with "Upper Echelon." His mythical story continues.[32]

Scott was very hands-on with *Rodeo*. In addition to overseeing the music and production elements, which to him felt more like designing than producing, Scott worked on everything from marketing to the album cover. He even designed his own Travis

Justin Bieber performs at the 2016 Brit Awards in London. Bieber contributed vocals on the song "Maria I'm Drunk," which appears on Scott's 2015 album, Rodeo.

Scott action figure, complete with a USB flash drive that had the album on it.

However, *Rodeo* was leaked early—and for free—without his meticulously planned rollout. Scott blamed Epic Records. "You were supposed to buy my album with an action figure and a USB. It would have been the illest [thing] ever," Scott told *Complex*. "This was the opportunity to raise the bar and set the standard. The whole packaging was meant to complete my story, but just because I'm young and they didn't trust the idea this . . . happens."[33]

Dreams Do Come True

Scott released his second studio album, *Birds in the Trap Sing McKnight*, in September 2016. This time it included a collaboration with Kid Cudi—two, in fact. Scott was overwhelmed because Cudi meant so much to him. He told *Rolling Stone*,

> In my whole career, all I wanted was acceptance from Kid Cudi. I don't care about *nothing else*! This dude saved my life. He kept me from doing a lot of [bad stuff] to myself, kept me on the right path. *That's* why I make music, *that's* why I go hard for the fans, *that's* why I tell security to move out of the way—'cause this dude gave me the passion, the information, the insight on how to grow up and be who you want to be.[34]

A coproduction of Grand Hustle and Epic, *Birds* claimed the number-one spot on the *Billboard* 200 the same week it came out. This was Scott's first number-one album. "Pick Up the Phone," a single with Young Thug and Georgia-born rapper Quavo, went double platinum. And "Goosebumps," featuring Kendrick Lamar, achieved five-times platinum status. *Birds* made multiple year-end top lists, including one for *Complex,* where it placed number five out of the top fifty best albums for 2016.

> "In my whole career, all I wanted was acceptance from Kid Cudi."[34]
>
> —Travis Scott

Scott also released *La Flame*, a documentary about Bird's Eye View, his concert tour for the album. The twenty-minute film gives Scott's fans a behind-the-scenes peek at his life on the road, in the studio, and just hanging out with friends.

Flying High

Fans and reviewers questioned Scott's enigmatic album title, *Birds in the Trap Sing McKnight*. Scott revealed it is a metaphor for feeling trapped in one's life and then breaking free and flying high. "[It's] basically about all my friends and growing up here [in Missouri City]," Scott told *Billboard*. "I'm not saying that it's a trap—we not in the . . . projects but it's like a social trap. It's a social connection trap from what you want to do and how you want to express yourself. I feel like everyone just gets constricted by their parents or just life."[35]

Scott definitely expressed himself both musically and creatively while promoting *Birds in the Trap Sing McKnight* for both Lamar's tour and his own Bird's Eye View tour. Part of that expression came in the form of a giant animatronic eagle that Scott designed himself. During his concerts, he danced and sang on the back of the bird (complete with flapping wings), which was suspended from the ceiling. Initially Scott wanted the bird to "fly" over the crowd, but the insurance costs were prohibitive.

For these performances, Scott reached back to his childhood. He asked what would have excited a young Jacques Webster. "I always just put myself in the fans' shoes," Scott told *GQ,* a men's magazine. "So if I was a fan right now, would I be hyped?"[36]

Still flying high, Scott ended 2016 with an appearance on Cudi's new album, *Passion, Pain & Demon Slayin'.* The December album was released to positive reviews, with many critics liking the Cudi-Scott pairing. Scott also agreed to sell his music catalogue (meaning the rights to his songs) to Grand Hustle Publishing/Universal Music Publishing Group. Jody Gerson, the CEO for Universal, told *Billboard,* "I've been chasing Travis Scott for years. His talent and ambitions are limitless. He's a rock star, as well as being a brilliant writer/producer."[37]

And there was one more childhood dream that Scott realized before the year was over. On December 27, he finally got his solo cover on *XXL Magazine*.

Scott continued to build his reputation in 2017. He announced he would be the executive producer on G.O.O.D. Music's *Cruel Winter*. The compilation album was heralded as the long-awaited sequel to *Cruel Summer* and was to showcase all the artists on West's label. The album was slated to be released in February 2017, but it was never released.

Delays are common in the music business. Scott had experienced multiple delays himself, especially with the release of *Rodeo.* This most likely informed his decision to launch his own record label, Cactus Jack Records. Scott said he formed the label mostly to provide a springboard for new artists. He explained in *Numéro*, a Paris fashion magazine, "I want to do for them what happened to me, but better. By better I mean no bull. . . . No lying to the artists about album release dates or the budgets of videos and albums."[38]

The Butterfly Effect

In May 2017, Scott released "Butterfly Effect," his first Cactus Jack project coproduced with Grand Hustle and Epic. The single—which was a teaser for his upcoming album *Astroworld*—was rumored to be about Kylie Jenner, whom Scott had started dating about a month earlier.

Scott's fans had been anticipating his third solo album ever since Scott first mentioned it in mid-2016. And "Butterfly Effect" did not disappoint. Even President Barack Obama revealed in a Facebook post that "Butterfly Effect" was on his 2017 playlist. The song was certified triple platinum. A week after "Butterfly Effect" was released, Scott's first two albums, *Rodeo* and *Birds in the Trap Sing McKnight,* were certified platinum—on the same day.

However, Scott's biggest success in 2017 happened through his collaboration on other artists' albums. On Drake's "Portland," Scott was featured along with Quavo. The single debuted at number nine on the Billboard Hot 100—Scott's first top-ten hit. Scott also worked with rhythm-and-blues singer Miguel on "Sky Walker." Both "Sky Walker" and "Portland" sold 2 million units each and were certified double platinum.

Scott followed this up by working with Quavo again. They formed a duo called Huncho Jack, the name being a reflection of Quavo's nickname ("Huncho") and Scott's new record label. Huncho Jack released its debut studio album, *Huncho Jack, Jack Huncho*, in December. The album peaked at number three on the *Billboard* 200 chart.

Astroworld

By most measures, Scott had already achieved success in his musical career. By 2018 he was earning millions and had his own record label and a string of *Billboard* hits. Life was good, but it was about to get even better. He was about to experience a new

"That's what [*Astroworld*'s] going to sound like, like taking an amusement park away from kids. We want it back."[39]

—Travis Scott

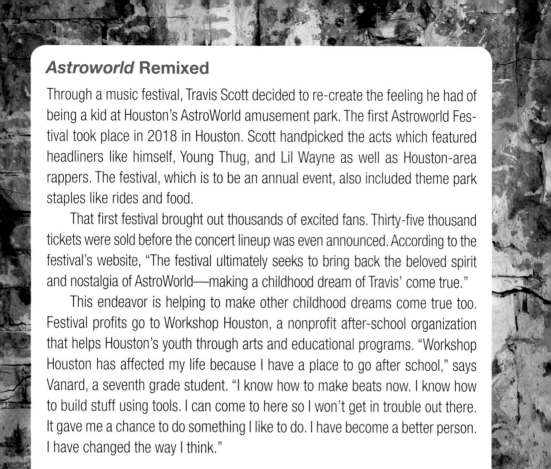

Astroworld Remixed

Through a music festival, Travis Scott decided to re-create the feeling he had of being a kid at Houston's AstroWorld amusement park. The first Astroworld Festival took place in 2018 in Houston. Scott handpicked the acts which featured headliners like himself, Young Thug, and Lil Wayne as well as Houston-area rappers. The festival, which is to be an annual event, also included theme park staples like rides and food.

That first festival brought out thousands of excited fans. Thirty-five thousand tickets were sold before the concert lineup was even announced. According to the festival's website, "The festival ultimately seeks to bring back the beloved spirit and nostalgia of AstroWorld—making a childhood dream of Travis' come true."

This endeavor is helping to make other childhood dreams come true too. Festival profits go to Workshop Houston, a nonprofit after-school organization that helps Houston's youth through arts and educational programs. "Workshop Houston has affected my life because I have a place to go after school," says Vanard, a seventh grade student. "I know how to make beats now. I know how to build stuff using tools. I can come to here so I won't get in trouble out there. It gave me a chance to do something I like to do. I have become a better person. I have changed the way I think."

Astroworld Festival, "About." https://astroworldfest.com.

Quoted in Workshop Houston, "What We Do." www.workshophouston.org.

stratosphere of success with *Astroworld*, the much-anticipated album based on Scott's beloved theme park of his youth. He shared on *GQ*, "They tore down AstroWorld to build more apartment space. That's what [*Astroworld*'s] going to sound like, like taking an amusement park away from kids. We want it back."[39]

Released on August 3, 2018, *Astroworld* achieved gold status in its first week. By September, it was platinum; and by January, it was double platinum. It was a critical and commercial success and Scott's second number-one album on the *Billboard* 200 chart, holding the top spot for three weeks.

Game On

Like most of the world, Travis Scott is a fan of *Game of Thrones*. In 2019 Scott posted a picture of himself on Instagram wearing a *Game of Thrones* suit of armor to promote *For the Throne,* a *Game of Thrones*–inspired soundtrack for the wildly popular HBO show. The photo features Scott posing in front of a Bentley, a luxury car, while wearing a breastplate over a chainmail shirt and a pair of leather pants. The album—and Scott's song "Power Is Power"—was produced by HBO and Columbia Records; it was released in April 2019 to coincide with the show's final season.

Buzz steadily built. By December, the album's single, "Sicko Mode," garnered Scott his first number-one hit on the Billboard Hot 100. It stayed in the top ten for thirty-two weeks, the first hip-hop song in history to do so. By the end of May 2019, it had gone six-times platinum, selling 6 million units. "Sicko Mode" was still in the Hot 100 (at number forty-two) by the end of June.

A Visionary Love Letter

Astroworld was seen as a love letter to Scott's hometown of Houston. As Sickamore, Scott's long-time A&R rep, explains, "The first album, *Rodeo,* was kind of his journey from Houston to L.A. This album is like, what do you do after you get the whole world? You go back home."[40]

Scott felt Houston did not get enough credit for its hip-hop community and the artists, like him, who came from there. Scott tried to remedy that by including references to Houston and its artists in the songs, along with samples and features from hometown artists. In keeping with his desire to avoid being pigeonholed into any one musical genre, the album featured Drake and Kid Cudi alongside pop artists like John Mayer, James Blake, and Stevie Wonder.

With the appearance of *Astroworld*, some were finally starting to get Scott's unique sound and his talent for bringing together disparate artists. As Ralph Bristout, a writer for the music cable network Revolt, explains,

> Through Travis' vision, all of this makes sense. After all, we don't call him rap's master collagist for no reason. . . . Scott has proven himself to be the heir to Kanye West in orchestrating all-star ensemble casts. He put Justin Bieber and Young Thug together for "Maria, I'm Drunk," a standout on 2015's *Rodeo*, and meshed well with Kid Cudi on "through the late night" on 2016's *Birds in the Trap Sing McKnight*. He is skilled at making the improbable, probable when it comes to creative decisions. On *Astroworld*, more than any of his prior releases, he masterfully connects worlds.[41]

Disappointment

Not everyone understands Scott's vision. Clearly, his 18 million followers on Instagram do. And even reviewers are starting to see his musical talents. One area that has eluded Scott has been industry recognition. According to Sickamore, *Astroworld* was a response to being ignored by the Grammy Awards for *Birds in the Trap Sing McKnight*. He told *Rolling Stone*, "That was a real dark day for us. We felt like we really worked hard and we really made a great album with *Birds* and we got snubbed. We went back and wanted to make an album that was undeniable. The Grammy snub was probably the best thing that happened to us."[42]

Although Scott and *Astroworld* were nominated for six Grammys in 2019, including Best Album and Best Rap Song for "Sicko Mode," he came up empty-handed. And that was despite his electric Grammy performance, during which he rapped in a cage and dove into a mosh pit.

Drake, who beat out Scott for several Grammys, summed up the music industry in his acceptance speech for Best Rap Song:

> This is a business where sometimes, you know, it's up to a bunch of people that might not understand, you know, what a mixed-race kid from Canada has to say, or a fly Spanish girl from New York [pointing to Cardi B]. . . . Or a brother from Houston right there, my brother Travis [pointing to Scott]. Look, the point is, you've already won. If you have people who are singing your songs word for word, if you're a hero in your hometown—look, look,—if there's people who have regular jobs, who are coming out in the rain, in the snow, spending their hard-earned money to buy tickets to come to your shows? You don't need this right here. I promise you. You already won.[43]

Wish You Were Here

Despite the disappointment of not winning a Grammy for *Astroworld*, Scott's Wish You Were Here Tour was an unqualified success. In line with his reputation for putting on frenetic shows, it featured fireworks and a working Ferris wheel. During the tour's first thirty-two concert dates, it grossed more than $34 million.

Scott is equally a creative and financial genius. He is known for his sense of style and has worked with many designers around the world. In 2017, for instance, he signed a multimillion-dollar deal to design footwear for Nike, an enterprise that helped boost him into the ranks of the fifteen highest-paid rappers on the planet for 2018.

When Nike released Scott's latest design on May 11, 2019—the Travis Scott x Air Jordan 1 "Cactus Jack" sneakers—Scott's fans went nuts. The limited edition Air Jordans, which featured a reversed Nike swoosh, interchangeable swooshes, and a secret pocket on the heel, sold out in a matter of hours, leaving many disappointed fans.

Scott, whose footwear of choice was Nike long before his collaboration with the sneaker giant, paid as much attention to

In 2019 Scott teamed with the multinational corporation Nike to create the Travis Scott x Air Jordan 1 "Cactus Jack" sneakers (pictured). The limited-edition sneakers sold out in a matter of hours.

detail with his design as he does with everything else. He said, "I looked at the making of this shoe the same way I make an album. I wanted it to tell a story about me."[44]

Scott also cut a deal with General Mills for his Travis Scott action figure to appear on Reese Puffs cereal boxes. After announcing the contract, he sold limited edition boxes that he designed himself. Each box cost fifty dollars, and they sold out in thirty seconds. General Mills has said it planned to release new Travis Scott cereal box designs in the future. Lauren Alvarez of *Forbes* sums up Scott's astronomical success:

> His business approach of little supply and high demand combined with his "cool kid" factor and impressionable merchandise has transitioned him to hip-hop elite. He integrates his music, merchandise, punk rock aura and overall *Astroworld* experience to create an invincible, authentic brand. Scott is redefining what it means to be a rapper today and is en route to dominating more than just the charts.[45]

REALITY BITES

Controversy seems to follow Travis Scott. And for someone who is extremely private, stories about his personal life have been plastered online and in print. Scott has been rumored to have dated everyone from superstar Rihanna to supermodel Kendall Jenner of the Kardashian clan. And in early 2017, he started a two-and-a-half-year relationship with Jenner's sister, model and billionaire makeup mogul Kylie Jenner, who is no stranger to the tabloids.

Scott and Jenner have no memory of how or when they met, but they had been traveling in the same circles for years. Plus, Scott's friend and mentor, Kanye West, is married to Jenner's sister Kim Kardashian. Neither of them claimed to have noticed the other before Coachella 2017—the annual music and arts festival in Indio, California, where Scott was performing on two consecutive weekends. The two hung out together, but this time friendship turned into something more. However, Coachella was only the second stop on Scott's Bird's Eye View tour, and he had about eight more weeks on the road. As Jenner explained in an interview with *GQ,* "He said, 'I'm going back on tour—what do we want to do about this?' Because obviously we liked each other. And I was like, 'I guess I'm going with you.'"[46] And she did.

Jenner shared that she and Scott had a lot of time together while traveling across the country. And being able to walk around cities freely with no fear of being recognized helped them get to know each other on a deeper level. In fact, ten months after Jenner and Scott started seeing each other, their daughter, Stormi, was born.

Scott has talked publicly of marriage to Jenner, stating she's "the one"—something that seemingly took him by surprise. Scott revealed to *Rolling Stone*, "Maybe, like, the first week, you don't know if it's real or a fling. Then the second week you're like, 'Whoa, I'm still talking to her, she's responding, I'm responding. We ain't run out of a thing to say.' And it got to a point where I was like, 'I need her with me to operate. She's that one.'"[47] At the time, Scott insisted that the two would tie the knot someday—all while dodging an allegation of having an affair that, according to some reports, almost broke them up.

No Show

Sometimes Scott's personal trials bleed into his work life. For example, in early 2019 gossip news site *TMZ* reported that Jenner had found some flirty messages from other women on Scott's phone and was convinced he was having an affair. According to *TMZ*, Scott and Jenner had a big fight. Scott, who was in the middle of his *Astroworld* tour, canceled his Buffalo, New York, concert at the last minute. The performance venue announced the cancellation was due to illness. However, *TMZ* reported that Scott canceled his performance so he could work through things with Jenner. Scott vehemently denied the rumor. Jenner has since admitted that she may have overreacted.

As for canceling his show, Scott does have a history of not showing up for concerts. Minnesota concert producer PJAM sued him in 2018, contending that Scott canceled a 2018 Minneapolis concert with short notice despite being paid $150,000 in advance. PJAM further claimed that Scott canceled because of the birth of his daughter two days earlier. Scott denied this and countersued, alleging PJAM failed to meet the conditions of its contract. In 2019 a jury found in favor of PJAM. Scott was ordered to pay the company close to $400,000.

Scott also failed to show up for a record release party promoting his first album, *Rodeo*. He was upset that *Rodeo* was released early, without the promotional items he had meticulously

Travis Scott (left) attends Paris Fashion Week in 2018 with (from left to right) Kylie Jenner, Kim Kardashian, and Kanye West. Scott and Jenner began dating in 2017 and have a daughter together.

packaged with it, and blamed his record company. A concert promoter, Empire Music Ventures, also sued Scott, alleging that he had signed a contract to headline the 2019 Rhythm, Wine & Blues Experience in California. According to Empire, right after they paid Scott a deposit of more than $200,000, Scott's people canceled the appearance. The company contends they were forced to cancel their festival due to lack of a headliner. It was later revealed that Scott was doing a concert in New York on the same night. Empire sued Scott for fraud and breach of contract. Scott's lawyers claimed Scott never agreed to do the concert and that the person who booked Scott was not his official booker. Eventually, Scott agreed to return the deposit and the lawsuit was dropped.

Working Out Differences

Scott has been the subject of other civil lawsuits. One involved a claim of copyright infringement. Part of making beats is sampling, or using bits of other artists' songs. This is normal in the hip-hop and rap world and is perfectly legal as long as the artist who owns the copyright of the song in question is paid for the use of it. In 2019 Scott was sued by DJ Paul of Three6Mafia. DJ Paul claimed the chant in Scott's "No Bystanders" song (on the *Astroworld* album) too closely resembled the hook of Three6Mafia's 1997 hit "Tear Da Club Up." However, when interviewed about the case by *Rolling Stone*, DJ Paul said the two sides were working out their differences.

Astroworld was at the center of another controversy. Shortly before the mega record was released, *TMZ* reported that California rapper Frank Ocean had sent a cease-and-desist order to Scott's management requesting that his contribution to the song "Carousel" be removed. Ocean claimed Scott changed his vocals without his permission. Ocean later praised Scott and his production on the song saying that he was just making a statement in support of transgender model Amanda Lepore.

Lepore's image did not make the final cut of the album cover. Ocean, along with many of Scott's fans, perceived the cut as evidence of transphobia and made him aware of it on social media. Scott addressed Lepore and his fans directly on Instagram. He said the cutting of her image was a misunderstanding, and he was working with his album designer to create a booklet of the original images from the album cover. "ASTROWORLD IS ABOUT LOVE AND EXPRESSION NOT HATE! Growing up I've been taught to accept everyone, not to cast people away but bring them into your home! I have nothing but respect for the LGBTQ community. I want to use my voice to make it clear that everyone on this planet is as equal and . . . awesome to the next."[48]

> "ASTROWORLD IS ABOUT LOVE AND EXPRESSION NOT HATE!"[48]
>
> —Travis Scott

Concert Chaos

Scott is known for his high-energy shows where he encourages his fans to rage, or party hard, and even become part of the show. Interaction between Scott and his fans at his concerts is part of the reason he is such a popular live performer; however, it has sometimes led to problems for the rapper.

For example, Scott had only been playing for about five minutes during the 2015 Lollapalooza music festival in Chicago when he encouraged fans to jump the security barricades and come to the stage. Security cut off Scott's music, and the concert was shut down. Scott was arrested and charged with disorderly conduct.

During Scott's 2017 Bird's Eye View tour at a New York City venue in April, fan Kyle Green was pushed off a balcony. Green said Scott encouraged people to dive off the balcony into the arms of the crowd below. According to Green, the frenzied crowd pushed forward, propelling him over the edge. Green was partially paralyzed by his injuries, which he claims were made worse by Scott's instructions to security to bring Green up on stage after he fell.

Fans eagerly wait for Scott to come onstage at the 2015 Lollapalooza Music Festival in Chicago. After encouraging the fans to jump over security barricades during his performance, Scott was arrested and charged with disorderly conduct.

Messing with Their Fans

Travis Scott and Kylie Jenner always liked to keep their fans guessing. Though the rapper and the model were not married—that anyone can confirm—the two often referred to each other as "wifey" and "hubby." In 2019 Jenner threw Scott a birthday party and presented him with a birthday cake inscribed with "Happy Birthday Hubby." Rumors circulated the two would get engaged during Scott's 2019 Super Bowl concert. No one knows whether it happened, but Scott posted a photo of Jenner backstage wearing a diamond ring.

Scott and Jenner also liked toying with fans about having a sibling for their daughter, Stormi. In February 2019, the two posed for a romantic photo on Jenner's Instagram account with the caption: "baby #2?"

"Kylie and Travis LOVE messing with us," *Seventeen* magazine editors Carolyn Twersky and Tamara Fuentes said at the time. "Seriously, they do it so much I think it's their favorite past time. While the rest of the world is embroiled in a discussion of 'are they engaged? Are they pregnant?' Kylie and Travis are probably looking through their Twitter feeds laughing at all the headlines struggling to unravel the rumors."

All this changed in October 2019 when the couple announced they were taking a break. Although they have appeared to have split up, could it just be another ploy?

Carolyn Twersky and Tamara Fuentes, "A Complete Timeline of Kylie Jenner and Travis Scott's Relationship," *Seventeen,* April 26, 2019. www.seventeen.com.

The *New York Post* reported that Green subsequently sued Scott, the security team, and Bowery Presents, the venue operator. Green further suggested that Bowery should have known about Scott's propensity for creating chaos at his events. A video of Scott encouraging a fan at the same concert to jump from a balcony went viral. Scott's lawyers issued a statement that their client was not responsible for Green's fall.

During the same concert tour in Rogers, Arkansas, a month later, Scott was arrested after he encouraged his fans to jump a security barrier and come up on the stage. Emboldened by Scott, dozens of fans stormed the stage while the rapper yelled at security to stand back and chanted, "We want rage."[49]

According to *People* magazine, Scott was arrested immediately following the concert. He was charged with inciting a riot, disorderly conduct, and endangering the welfare of a minor. Keith Foster, a spokesperson for the Rogers police department, said, "During the concert, [Scott] encouraged people to rush the stage and bypass security protocols to ensure concert goer safety. During the rush to the stage several people were injured, including an employee from the security company hired to help monitor and control the crowd, and a member of the police department."[50]

Scott's loyal fans took to social media, tweeting hashtags like "#FreeTravisScott and #FreeLaFlame. After Scott was released from jail, he had a flash sale on his website, selling limited edition T-shirts featuring his mug shot on the front and the phrase "Free the Rage" on the back. *TMZ* reported that Scott pled guilty to disorderly conduct in exchange for having the other two charges dismissed.

Scott has been frustrated by these experiences. His goal, he says, is to create a great show for his fans. In 2017 *Rolling Stone* asked Scott if the arrests had inspired a change in his behavior during concerts. Scott replied, "It hasn't. People gotta understand, sometimes [things get] out of control. I'm not trying to cause no harm—I just perform. . . . I just wanna bring the stage to, like, the masses. I feel I have a show for the masses."[51]

> **"I feel I have a show for the masses."[51]**
>
> —Travis Scott

Peer Pressure

Scott has, at times, gotten himself in trouble with his peers as well. Singer Nicki Minaj has accused Scott of manipulating chart status by offering bundled products like action figures and hoodies along with digital downloads of his music. A month after *Astroworld* was released, the album went platinum. That did not please Minaj. As Shawn Grant of the *Source*, a hip-hop magazine, explains, "Travis and *Astroworld* were heavy in the news as it was in an intense battle with Nicki Minaj and her latest album, *Queen*, for the number one spot. Travis held on to the top position but received some fiery words from Nicki stating that he did everything possible from selling merch to using his child to promote the work."[52]

Scott was also criticized for taking part in the 2019 Super Bowl halftime show. At the time, there was anger over how the National Football League (NFL) had treated San Francisco 49ers quarterback Colin Kaepernick. Kaepernick had protested police shootings involving African Americans by taking a knee during the playing of the national anthem at his games. Other prominent musical acts, including Jay-Z, Rihanna, Cardi B, and Pink, had reportedly turned down the famed halftime show, and Jay-Z and the Reverend Al Sharpton spoke out against Scott's performing.

To protest police brutality against African Americans, San Francisco 49ers quarterback Colin Kaepernick kneels during the national anthem prior to an NFL game against the Seattle Seahawks in 2016.

Scott considered the comments but did the show anyway. It put him squarely in the eye of mainstream America. Before accepting the job, however, he asked the NFL to donate $500,000 to the Dreams Corps, a social justice organization. Scott then put out a statement: "I back anyone who takes a stand for what they believe in. I know being an artist that it's in my power to inspire. So before confirming the Super Bowl Halftime performance, I made sure to partner with the NFL on this important donation. I am proud to support Dream Corps and the work they do that will hopefully inspire and promote change."[53]

Scott also faced criticism for agreeing to perform at the 2019 Grammy Awards. Several rap performers, including Drake and

Hometown Hero

In September 2018, Sandra Vasquez—a student from Dwight D. Eisenhower High School in Houston, Texas—posted an image on Twitter to Travis Scott. The image was a mockup of a shirt the students designed for their 2019 senior class. It featured artwork from Scott's records, which Vasquez was seeking permission to use.

Scott responded on Twitter by saying he would design the seniors' shirts himself. And he was true to this word. Three months later the school received their shirts, which he revealed on social media with the caption, "Flame always delivers for the kids."

The original design featured a happy face superimposed over the Earth as well as the tagline from his *Astroworld* tour, "Wish You Were Here." On the back of the t-shirt Scott wrote the phrase "Enjoy the ride," along with his signature.

The Eisenhower students were thrilled. In response, Vasquez posted on social media, "We love Travis and all he does for Houston."

That is not the first time Scott has shown some love to his hometown. In 2017 he hosted a turkey drive for Thanksgiving following Hurricane Harvey.

Quoted in Renz Ofiaza, "Travis Scott Actually Designed Graduation Merch for a Houston High School," Highsnobiety, December 17, 2018. www.highsnobiety.com.

Quoted in Trent Fitzgerald, "Travis Scott Designs Senior T-Shirts for Students at Houston High School," *XXL Magazine*, December 17, 2018. www.xxlmag.com.

Lamar, had declined to take part. They were protesting the lack of hip-hop acts taking home awards in the top music categories.

Using His Power for Good

Scott has almost 20 million social media followers. He knows he has the ability to influence people, and he speaks up about things he believes in—although sometimes Scott's opinions can be quite polarizing. During a 2014 radio show on station Hot 97, Scott suggested that Michael Brown Jr., the unarmed black teen who was killed by a white police officer in Ferguson, Missouri, "deserved" his fate:

I'm kind of angry, so many black people are acting like fake activists. . . . I'm not saying he deserved to get killed, but I'm not saying that he didn't deserve to pay for consequences he probably inflicted. I know we're like "fed up" with whatever is going on in culture, but at the same time you gotta just stop putting yourself in positions where you're continuously having this situation go down.[54]

Scott's comments were seen as victim blaming and outraged many of his fans.

However, for the most part, Scott tries to use his celebrity for good. For example, in May 2019, in response to Alabama's new restrictive abortion laws, he donated concert profits from the merchandise sales to Planned Parenthood, a nonprofit organization that offers abortions and women's reproductive care. And in October 2018, Scott campaigned for fellow Texan Beto O'Rourke, the Democratic candidate for the US Senate in the 2018 midterm election and encouraged his fans to vote: "All the kids, we've just got to go out and hit these polls. From 18 and up, we can change the world."[55] And maybe that is all Scott has ever wanted—for his voice to be heard.

Introduction: The Voice

1. Quoted in Nadeska Alexis, "Travis Scott Sets It Straight: 'I'm Not Hip Hop,'" *MTV News*, June 25, 2013. www.mtv.com.
2. Jeff Miers, "Travis Scott and the Rise of Hip-Hop-as-Text-Message," *Gusto* (blog), *Buffalo News,* February 27, 2019. https://buffalonews.com.
3. Quoted in Israel Daramola, "Watch Travis Scott Perform 'Sicko Mode,' Talk About His Daughter on *Ellen*," *Spin*, November 12, 2018. www.spin.com.
4. Miers, "Travis Scott and the Rise of Hip-Hop-as-Text-Message."
5. Andy Kellman, "Artist Biography," *AllMusic*. www.allmusic.com.
6. Quoted in Lawrence Schlossman, "Idol Worship," *Complex*, December 2015–January 2016. www.complex.com.
7. Zach Quiñones, "Millennials Have Found Their Dr. Dre and His Name Is Travis Scott," *Medium*, August 14, 2018. https://medium.com.
8. Zack O'Malley Greenburg and Natalie Robehmed, eds., "Top 30 Under 30: Music, Topping Charts and Shifting Culture," *Forbes*, 2018. www.forbes.com.

Chapter 1: Finding His Way

9. Quoted in Insanul Ahmed, "Who Is Travi$ Scott?," *Complex,* October 3, 2012. www.complex.com.
10. Quoted in Ahmed, "Who Is Travi$ Scott?"
11. Quoted in Jonah Weiner, "Travis Scott: Hip Hop's King of Chaos," *Rolling Stone,* September 25, 2017. www.rollingstone.com.
12. Kathy Iandoli, "Blessed Up," *XXL Magazine*, December 2016–January 2017. www.xxlmag.com.
13. Quoted in Ahmed, "Who Is Travi$ Scott?"
14. Quoted in Schlossman, "Idol Worship."
15. Quoted in Jonah Weiner, "Travis Scott: In Orbit with Rap's Newest Superstore," *Rolling Stone*, December 20, 2018. www.rollingstone.com.

16. Quoted in Schlossman, "Idol Worship."
17. Quoted in Ahmed, "Who Is Travi$ Scott?"
18. Quoted in Ahmed, "Who Is Travi$ Scott?"
19. Quoted in Eric Brain, "Producer Anthony Kilhoffer Talks Kanye West & Travis Scott in 'Kids Take Over' Interview," *Hypebeast*, April 24, 2019. https://hypebeast.com.
20. Quoted in Ahmed, "Who Is Travi$ Scott?"
21. Quoted in Ahmed, "Who Is Travi$ Scott?"

Chapter 2: The Grand Hustle

22. Quoted in Brain, "Producer Anthony Kilhoffer Talks Kanye West & Travis Scott in 'Kids Take Over' Interview."
23. Quoted in Ahmed, "Who Is Travi$ Scott?"
24. Quoted in Jake Woolf, "Travi$ Scott—the Design of Music," *Hypebeast*, January 29, 2013. https://hypebeast.com.
25. Quoted in Elias Leight, "Travis Scott Talks 'Straight to the Meat' Second Album," *Rolling Stone*, September 2, 2016. www.rollingstone.com.
26. Quoted in Rob Markmam, "Kanye West and T.I. Give Travis Scott 'the Best of Both Worlds,'" *MTV News*, May 9, 2013. www.mtv.com.
27. Quiñones, "Millennials Have Found Their Dr. Dre and His Name Is Travis Scott."
28. Frazier Tharpe, "I Tried Not to Die at Travi$ Scott and Young Thug's Show Last Night," *Complex*, March 13, 2015. www.complex.com.

Chapter 3: Astronomical Success

29. Quoted in Kathy Iandoli, "T.I. Talks *Entourage* Cameo, 'Finished New Album,' & Working with Travis Scott," *Billboard*, June 8, 2015. www.billboard.com.
30. Quoted in Nadeska Alexis, "Travi$ Scott Shed Tears When He Met Kid Cudi," *MTV News*, March 23, 2015. www.mtv.com.
31. Quoted in Alexis, "Travi$ Scott Shed Tears When He Met Kid Cudi."

32. Edwin Ortiz, "The Best Albums of 2015," *Complex*, December 1, 2015. www.complex.com.

33. Quoted in Schlossman, "Idol Worship."

34. Quoted in Leight, "Travis Scott Talks 'Straight to the Meat' Second Album."

35. Quoted in Adele Platon, "Travis Scott Shares Inspiration Behind 'Birds in the Trap Sing McKnight' Album, Announces Third LP Title," *Billboard*, May 18, 2016. www.billboard.com.

36. Quoted in Jake Woolf, "Travis Scott on the Show That's So Crazy, It Caused a Riot," *GQ*, May 15, 2017. www.gq.com.

37. Quoted in Ashely Iasimone, "Travis Scott Inks Worldwide Deal with Universal Music Publishing Group," *Billboard*, September 12, 2016. www.billboard.com.

38. Quoted in Olivier Joyard, "Travis Scott Launches His Label Cactus Jack Records and Other Revelations," *Numéro*, March 6, 2017. www.numero.com.

39. Quoted in Paul Flynn, "Travis Scott Doesn't Fall on Stage, He Flies," *GQ*, March 14, 2017. www.gq.com.

40. Quoted in Elias Leight, "How Travis Scott (and His A&R) Got John Mayer, Drake and Stevie Wonder on the Same Album," *Rolling Stone*, August 7, 2018. www.rollingstone.com.

41. Ralph Bristout, "7 Quick Takeaways from Travis Scott's 'Astroworld,'" Revolt, August 4, 2018. https://revolt.tv.

42. Quoted in Leight, "How Travis Scott (and His A&R) Got John Mayer, Drake and Stevie Wonder on the Same Album."

43. Quoted in Chris Richards, "Drake Was the Unlikely Source for the Grammy's Biggest Moment of Truth," *Washington Post*, February 11, 2019. www.washingtonpost.com.

44. Quoted in Chris Danforth, "The Complete Beginner's Guide to Every Travis Scott Sneaker Collaboration," Highsnobiety, April 3, 2019. www.highsnobiety.com.

45. Lauren Alvarez, "How Travis Scott Scored a No. 1 Album 4 Months After Its Release Date," *Forbes*, December 4, 2018. www.forbes.com.

Chapter 4: Reality Bites

46. Quoted in Mark Anthony Green, "Kylie Jenner and Travis Scott on Love, Making It Work, and the Kardashian Curse," *GQ*, July 17, 2018. www.gq.com.

47. Quoted in Weiner, "Travis Scott: In Orbit with Rap's Newest Superstar."

48. Quoted in Jessica Vacco-Bolanos, "Travis Scott Addresses Album Controversy over Transgender Model Amanda Lepore, 'Sorry for the Misunderstanding,'" *US Magazine*, August 5, 2018. www.usmagazine.com.

49. Quoted in Daniel Kreps, "Travis Scott Arrested After Fans Storm Lollapalooza Stage," *Rolling Stone*, August 3, 2015. www.rollingstone.com.

50. Quoted in Stephanie Petit and Aurelie Corinthios, "Travis Scott Arrested for Allegedly Inciting Riot at Arkansas Concert," *People*, May 14, 2017. https://people.com.

51. Quoted in Weiner, "Travis Scott: Hip Hop's King of Chaos."

52. Shawn Grant, "Travis Scott's 'Astroworld' Is Now Platinum," *Source*, August 28, 2018. http://thesource.com.

53. Quoted in Bre Williams, "The Real Reason Travis Scott Agreed to Perform at the Super Bowl Halftime Show," Showbiz Cheat Sheet, January 14, 2019. www.cheatsheet.com.

54. Quoted in Paul Meara, "Uh Oh, Twitter Unearthed Travis Scott Interview Where He Makes Anti-Black Comments Following Super Bowl Controversy," BET, December 22, 2018. www.bet.com.

55. Quoted in Brendan Klinkenberg, "Travis Scott Voices Support for Beto O'Rourke at Houston Rally," *Rolling Stone*, October 29, 2018. www.rollingstone.com.

Important Events in the Life of Travis Scott

1991 or 1992
Scott is born Jacques Berman Webster II on April 30 in Houston, Texas.

1997
Scott and his family move to Missouri City, a Houston suburb.

2005
AstroWorld, a theme park that was a symbol of Scott's childhood, closes.

2008
Scott forms a duo called the Graduates with Chris Holloway; they release an EP to MySpace.

2009
Scott forms a duo called the Classmates with Jason Eric; they release their first of two music projects.

2011
Scott drops out of college and moves to New York, then to Los Angeles.

2012
Scott releases the video "Lights (Love Sick)," signs his first record contract with Epic Records, and signs with Kanye West's G.O.O.D. Music as a producer.

2013
Scott signs with T.I.'s Grand Hustle Records; he also releases *Owl Pharaoh*, his first mixtape.

2014
His second mixtape, *Days Before Rodeo,* is released.

2015

Scott releases his debut studio album, *Rodeo.*

2016

Scott releases his second studio album, *Birds in the Trap Sing McKnight*.

2017

Scott launches his own record label, Cactus Jack Records.

2018

Scott releases his third solo album, *Astroworld*; he and Kylie Jenner celebrate the birth of their daughter, Stormi Webster.

2019

Scott performs at both the Super Bowl halftime show and the Grammy Awards, where he had been nominated for six Grammys.

Books

Judy Dodge Cummings, *Hip-Hop Culture*. Minneapolis: ABDO, 2018.

Stuart A. Kallen, *Rap and Hip-Hop*. San Diego: Reference-Point, 2020.

Marcia Amidon Lusted, *Hip-Hop Music*. Minneapolis: ABDO, 2018.

New York Times Editorial Staff, eds., *Influential Hip-Hop Artists: Kendrick Lamar, Nicki Minaj and Others*. New York: Rosen, 2019.

Internet Sources

Constance Grady, "The Super Bowl Halftime Show Controversies, Explained," Vox, February 3, 2019. www.vox.com.

Althea Legaspi, "Travis Scott, the Weeknd, the National Tapped for 'Game of Thrones' Soundtrack," *Rolling Stone*, April 9, 2019. www.rollingstone.com.

Paul Meara, "Uh Oh: Twitter Unearthed Travis Scott Interview Where He Makes Anti-Black Comments Following the Super Bowl Controversy," BET, December 22, 2018. www.bet.com.

Matt Miller, "The Super Bowl Halftime Show Is Becoming a Real Mess for Travis Scott and the NFL," *Esquire*, January 16, 2019. www.esquire.com.

Jonah Weiner, "Travis Scott: In Orbit with Rap's Newest Superstar," *Rolling Stone*, December 20, 2018. www.rollingstone.com.

INDEX

Cover: hurricanehank/iStock

6: Dafydd Owen/Retna/Avalon.red/Newscom
9: Associated Press
12: Jim Ruymen/UPI/Newscom
17: Marek Masik/Shutterstock.com
21: Kevork Djansekzian/Reuters/Newscom
23: Associated Press
29: Sky Cinema/Shutterstock.com
32: Matt Crossick/Zuma Press/Newscom
35: Associated Press
41: Courtesy of Nike/Mega/Newscom
44: Laurent VU/Sipa/Newscom
46: Associated Press
49: Associated Press